How To Preserve Eggs
Methods of Storing Eggs

by H.H. Stoddard

with an introduction by Jackson Chambers

Self Reliance Books

Get more historic titles on animal and stock breeding, gardening and old fashioned skills by visiting us at:

http://selfreliancebooks.blogspot.com/

Introduction

I am pleased to present yet another title in the "Poultry" series.

This volume is entitled "How to Preserve Eggs" in 1885.

The work is in the Public Domain and is re-printed here in accordance with Federal Laws.

Though this work is a century old it contains much information on poultry that is still pertinent today.

As with all reprinted books of this age that are intended to perfectly reproduce the original edition, considerable pains and effort had to be undertaken to correct fading and sometimes outright damage to existing proofs of this title. At times, this task is quite monumental, requiring an almost total "rebuilding" of some pages from digital proofs of multiple copies. Despite this, imperfections still sometimes exist in the final proof and may detract from the visual appearance of the text.

I hope you enjoy reading this book as much as I enjoyed making it available to readers again.

Jackson Chambers

Kellerstrass Farm
Arthur Oscar Schilling
1907

2

HOW TO PRESERVE EGGS.

EGGS.

THE egg contains all the principles essential to the growth of the body, though not every chemical substance that the stomach will take and use for the development of bodily organs. It does not contain a large portion of starch. Milk is the food provided by nature for the young, and affords all the elements necessary in building up and sustaining the body during the stage for which it is provided. So the egg contains enough of nitrogenous substance, oil or fatty elements, water, lime, etc., to make the frame, the flesh, and all the tiny organs of the chicken, covering all with a downy garment that answers for the time, in part, as a protection.

The shell of an egg is not air tight. The pores of the shell admit air sufficient, during the period of incubation, to produce those changes necessary for the development of the chicken. This is a necessity of the case; but when we come to the preservation of eggs for culinary purposes these pores in the shell, admitting the atmosphere, are what bring about a putrid condition, and cause what was very superior as an article of food to be entirely useless — a total loss.

It seems that eggs are not designed by nature, or produced for food, but for reproduction. They keep better than the manna of the wilderness; yet, if we watch the process, we see that when the fowl has completed her "laying" she immediately commences sitting, and therefore there is no need, in the course of nature, for the eggs to keep in prime condition for more than two or three weeks.

Man, by selection of the most fruitful specimens for breeding, by affording protection and food, also by stimulating, has produced a habit in the domestic fowl of producing more eggs annually than are necessary for incubation. The eggs are taken away from the nest day by day, and the hen keeps on laying and cackling till she has produced more than three fowls of her size can cover with extended wings. She needs but a dozen; cunning man takes the balance for his breakfast table.

Spring and early summer are the seasons — a period of about five months — when our domestic fowls produce abundance of eggs, even more than required for sitting and to fill the current demand. There is a surplus. Eggs are cheap. If pressed upon the market fast as produced, the price gets reduced down to a ruinously low figure, and the poultryman gets discouraged; hence an inquiry comes every year from every part of the country, "What is the best method of preserving eggs?" "Is there a possibility of keeping eggs perfectly fresh from the time of plenty to the time of scarcity?"

The desire to answer our many correspondents, giving them all that has been discovered and all that is worth knowing on the subject, has prompted to the commencement of another book in our series on poultry and subjects pertaining thereto. And now let us inquire diligently how to keep eggs. We find that there has been no lack of experiment in this matter. One writer asserts, that air enters when an egg has been long kept, and brings about its putrefaction, and that giving a coating of some impervious material to the shell, or filling up the pores with oily substance, the egg will keep for an almost indefinite period. This is true in part, but there are other important conditions that should not be left out of consideration.

A lot of eggs kept in a high temperature, or in a temperature that varies from high to low, as in our American climate, will in a short time depreciate in quality and in a few weeks be worthless for culinary purposes, be they sealed ever so carefully. The *position* of eggs for keeping is also important. Eggs lying on their sides will soonest decay. It is important that the membrane which surrounds the yolk keeping it in its globular shape be kept intact. The breaking of this membrane causes the mixture of the yolk with the albuminous matter surrounding it. When an egg lies on its side for many days the yolk settles to the lower side, the membrane which surrounds it coming in contact with the lining of the shell. This hastens the giving way of the membrane. The yolk should be surrounded with the white as evenly as possible; thus it will be kept in a globular shape, and there will be no uneven strain on the membrane. Who has not noticed in cutting a hard-boiled egg the yolk at one side and the air space pressed nearly opposite? The egg laid unchanged too long on one side, and was boiled none too soon; for before long it would have been a "bad egg," and that is the very opposite of the article commonly denominated a "fresh egg."

Eggs ought to make an important part of the diet of the young, the delicate, and the dyspeptic. The laborer also finds out that there is something in eggs that sustains him in his toil. If boiled hard they are handy to carry, only need a little salt for their preparation, and are never estimated much short of meat in nutritive qualities. Ah, yes! a fresh egg is better than salt meat; and a *fresh egg* is one *lately laid*, and so it will be to the end of the world. There is a difference in the quality of fresh eggs as there is in milk. This may be accounted for by the breed, or by the food with which the fowls have been supplied. Some eggs appear to contain more water than others, and less of oily matter in the yolk; also, some have a richer *flavor* than others. When fowls have enjoyed a recess of weeks in winter, receiving good feed, all the tissues of the body get filled up, and the first dozen or score laid have all the richness that comes of good material. Especially is this the case when fowls have the liberty of the farm, and get not only good food, but a variety.

As the special object of the writer is to give the best methods of preserving eggs for food, and to relate the experience of numerous persons who have made experiments with this object in view, it is only just and right that we start out with a true knowledge of the structure of eggs, and the material of which they are composed. The preservation of beef and pork to an indefinite time is effected by a low temperature. Eggs may be so preserved for a long time, care being taken not to freeze; also, to seal perfectly to prevent evaporation and the ingress of air. But it is by the use of *salt* that meats are commonly preserved. We all know how much of good quality and flavor is lost by this process. The palatable juices of the meat go out as the salt goes in. Eggs may be preserved with salt, but the hardening and depreciation of quality is much the same. If we study the nature of an egg we are inclined to the opinion that it is not made to be kept like wine.

Eggs have been aptly called "hen fruit." The ovary of a fowl presents what appears like a cluster of fruit not yet mature. The process of fecundation is wonderful, but that is not necessary to the production of an egg. An apple falls not from the tree without a previous contact of pollen with the stigma, in a blossom; but our "hen fruit" falls into the nest, it may be, without impregnation, a perfect egg to all appearance, just as good for food, just as good to keep, as though it contained within its shell the possibility of a chicken.

The ovary of the hen is where the germs cluster, and here is the beginning of every egg-centre. In a laying hen the yolks are found in every stage of development. This growth or secretion comes from the blood by means of the ovary. The yolks are each enveloped by a sac that holds them in form till perfected, and ready to break away from the ovary. About the time of fecundation this sac becomes thinner and weaker, especially about the largest circumference of the yolk, and finally breaks asunder. The germ and yolk, enveloped in a membrane exceedingly delicate, now enter another organ called the

oviduct.   This is a flexible passage, nearly two feet long
in some fowls.   During the laying period this organ
receives a liberal supply of blood.   The organ is extended
and active, the amount and quality of its secretions being
truly wonderful.   As the yolk enters the upper end of
the passage, preserving its rotundity, it begins to receive
an envelope of albuminous substance — the white — a secretion from the oviduct, apparently not constant but period-
ical, as it is formed in layers.   These layers appear
distinctly in the white of a boiled egg, and may in some
cases be separated.   The imperfect egg moves along
downward, probably stopping at intervals, receiving when
at the middle, or about the middle, of the passage, a
secretion that forms a covering or skin, in two layers.
This includes the yolk and white, and a bubble of highly
oxygenated air, which is found at the large end, not in
immediate contact with the egg, but between the two
layers of skin.   Thus is formed a bag containing all the
elements necessary to form the body of a chick.   Only
one thing more is necessary to carry out the plan — a
shell.   In the lower part of the oviduct the imperfect
egg receives its hard outer covering of calcareous substance, rendering it fit and handy to be carried or kept.
This is the mechanism of nature.   Does it not appear
like a contrivance?   And who runs the machine?   The
hen takes no thought of this ; not as much as of the
worm that wriggles in her crop.   These formations of
germs, and all that belongs to the egg, from the germ to
the downy chicks,—how wonderful !   There are some little
points that the best philosopher skips over, because forsooth,
darkness covers them, and they are past finding out.

And now we have the egg. Man has dominion; he gives what he chooses to the sitting hen, or to the incubator, and takes the balance of *good eggs* for the table. One of the most important arts among mankind is the art of preserving food so that the surplus that exists at one time, or in one country, may be saved and utilized. We can hardly realize the amount of suffering that is prevented by this. With modern inventions, and methods of transportation, famine is avoided.

We have just been considering the ways by which eggs are produced, and the substance entering their formation. Eggs are highly nitrogenous. There is a flavor to the fresh article that may not be described, but is a luxury; missed when you have the egg without the flavor. Sometimes we hear people saying that this recipe, or that method, will preserve eggs so that they will be just as good at the end of six months or a year as when newly laid. This is in the region of extravagance. Flesh and fish are depreciated by any methods of preservation. The same is the case with fruits, if we except quinces and two or three other kinds.

In the methods of keeping eggs which we present in these pages, we shall endeavor to accumulate all of experiment and discovery that has been brought to light up to the present time. The reader will, of course, discriminate. Some of these methods are best only for the household, others for the person who would pack large numbers to be sent to distant markets.

There is abundant evidence that eggs may be kept many months in such good state of preservation as to make valuable food, and a knowledge of the methods of doing this is worth something to the man who nas eggs to keep.

SALT, LIME, ETC.

At the Birmingham Poultry Show, England, prizes were offered for the best eggs that had been kept two months. The eggs were tested by breaking one of each lot, into a clean saucer; also by boiling one of each lot. The eggs that had been preserved in lime water, it was found on breaking them, presented cloudy whites. Eggs preserved by rubbing over with beeswax and oil showed thin, watery whites.

Eggs that stood best the test of boiling and which gained the first prize had been simply packed in common salt. These had lost little, if any, by evaporation, had good, consistent albumen, and were pleasant to the taste. The exhibit which took the second prize was served as follows : Melt one part of white wax to two parts spermaceti, boil and mix thoroughly; or two parts clarified suet to one of wax and two of spermaceti. Take new-laid eggs, rub with antiseptic salt or fine rice starch. Wrap each egg in fine tissue paper, putting the broad end downward; screw the paper tightly at the top, leaving an inch to hold it by. Dip each egg rapidly into the fat heated to 100 degrees. Withdraw and leave to cool. Pack broad end downward in dry, white sand or saw-dust. The judges were inclined to believe that had the trial been for a longer period than two months, this latter method would perhaps have proven the better of the two. The eggs were excellent, and on stripping off the waxed paper the shells presented the clean, fresh appearance of newly-laid eggs.

A correspondent of the English *Live Stock Journal* gives the following recipe: "To every gallon of water, add a breakfast cupful of quick-lime, and a breakfast cupful of salt. Put the lime in a flat-bottomed oval earthenware pan with enough of the water to slake it; when cold, add the rest of the water and the salt, and mix well. Put the eggs in the day they are laid. I rarely have a broken egg, if the eggs are sound when put in. I think the salt prevents the lime spoiling the shells much, up to six months; a longer time is apt to make thin shells."

The *American Agriculturist* gives the following: "Eggs may be kept from late summer or autumn well into the winter, or even spring, but it is next to impossible to deceive the dealers, and very few customers are deceived by them. 'Limed eggs' have their regular market quotations throughout the winter, and usually sell at one-quarter to one-sixth less than fresh ones. They are limed by packing them into barrels or smaller casks, point down, and pouring on them the water from lime slacked with brine, to a thin milky consistency, using just enough to cover the eggs, so that the next layer can be conveniently placed upon these and then more lime water added. When the cask is full, the eggs must be covered with a cloth and this spread over thickly with the pasty lime, and then if the water evaporates, or if the pasty lime cakes and cracks, more water must be added. It is essential that the eggs should be perfectly fresh, clean and sweet when packed, or the whole lot will go wrong. There is, probably, no better way of keeping eggs for market than this. For family use they may be greased, dipped in hot paraffine wax, scalded, and perhaps preserved in other ways. The lime and salt liquid imparts no flavor, and does not deface the egg, which, when offered for sale, has a slight chalky appearance, foreign to and distinguishes it from a fresh-laid egg."

And here follows the experience of two English writers in keeping eggs for family use:

"I slake the lime in an old iron boiler, making it about the consistency of treacle. I let it stand thus for fourteen days, with water an inch deep on the top. Then take an earthen pan, put some of the lime in it, three inches deep, and put the eggs in the same day as laid, and push them under the lime Always keep a little water on the top of the lime. This will keep it soft, and exclude the air. In this way I have kept eggs for thirteen months for trial, but we always keep them from four to seven months, and never find any bad ones. I have laid down about 500 this season, and do so every season. I only keep Dark Brahmas at present, but have during the last forty-six years tried nearly every breed."

"In the month of September I bought an ordinary basket of eggs, about 150, at 1d. each. I put them, the large end downwards, in a large upright earthenware jar, with sufficient dried salt between each egg to prevent contact, and filled the jar quite full with salt, covered with bladder, putting them away in a very dry place. In the following month of March those that were left were perfectly good and sweet, weighing on an average eight to the 1 lb."

A Massachusetts correspondent of the *Western Rural*

gives his experience on this subject, as follows: "I am anxious one and all should know the secret of keeping eggs a year or more in as perfect a state as when laid, with this exception, that when they are beaten up they are more brittle than new-laid eggs. I am giving you a recipe that has been in use by men who have brought eggs to the Boston market from the State of Maine for the last thirty years, and who have tested the same with more than a million dozen of eggs, in the time mentioned, and know of what they speak. It is as follows: Take five quarts of rock salt, five pounds of unslaked lime and a quarter of a pound of cream of tartar; dissolve in four pails of water, which makes sufficient pickle for a barrel of eggs. Eggs are always to be kept under the pickle. I have used the same for preserving our eggs for family use for the last twenty years, and am giving conclusion from experience. To which we would add, however, that although this may preserve eggs in good condition, it will not save those eggs that have been left in the nest for twenty-four hours, and have been kept warm during that time by hens sitting on them."

To the above should be added that all the eggs, besides being perfectly fresh, should be perfectly sound. Unslaked lime injures the shells.

For the benefit of those who wish to preserve eggs on a large scale, we insert the method that has been indorsed by the *American National Butter, Cheese and Egg Association:* "One bushel of lime, eight quarts of salt, and 250 quarts of water. Slake the lime with a portion of the water, then add the balance of the water and the salt. Stir well three or four times at intervals, and let it stand until well settled and cold. Either dip or draw off the clear pickle into the cask or vat in which it is intended to preserve the eggs. When the cask or vat is filled to a depth of eighteen inches begin to put in the eggs, and when they lie about one foot deep, spread over them some pickle that is a little milky in appearance, made so by stirring up some of the very light lime particles that settled last, and continue doing this as each foot of eggs is added. The object of this is to have the fine lime particles drawn into the pores of the shells, as they will be by a kind of inductive process and thereby completely seal the eggs. Care should be taken not to get too much of the lime in; that is, not enough to settle and stick to the shells of the eggs and render them difficult to clean when taken out. I believe that the chief cause of the thin, watery whites in limed eggs is that they are not properly sealed in the manner described. Of course, another cause is the putting into the pickle old, stale eggs, that have thin, watery whites. When the eggs are within about four inches of the end of the cask or vat, cover them with factory cloth and spread on two or three inches of the lime that settles in making the pickle; and it is of the utmost importance that the pickle be kept continually up over this lime. A thin basin, holding about six to eight dozen eggs, punched quite full of inch holes, edge muffled with leather, and a suitable handle about three feet long attached, will be found convenient for putting the eggs into the pickle. Fill the basin with eggs, put both under the pickle and turn the eggs out; they will go to the bottom without breaking. Vats built in a cellar around the walls, with about half their depth below the surface, and four or five feet deep, six feet long and four feet wide, are usually considered the best for preserving eggs in, although many use and prefer large tubs made of wood. The place in which the vats are built or the tubs set should be clean and sweet, free from all bad odors, and where a steady, low temperature can be obtained. The lower the better; that is, down to any point above freezing."

To lime a few eggs for home use, Fanny Field gives a recipe: One pint of salt, one pint of lime and four gallons of boiling water. When cold put into stone jars, or anything that will not absorb the liquid, then with a dish let the eggs down into it so that they will roll out without cracking the shell; for if the shell is cracked the egg will spoil. Keep covered in a good place. And here, to avoid repetition, I will say, that no matter what method you use, the eggs should always be kept covered and in a dry place where a "steady, low temperature can be maintained"—the lower the better, provided it does not reach the freezing point. Eggs will not keep well in a damp, musty cellar, or in a room where the mercury waltzes up and down all the way from 40 degrees above zero to 90-in-the-shade. And the eggs must be fresh to begin with. I had the best success with eggs that were packed every day as soon as gathered from the nests.

The same writer discourses, in a general way, on this subject, as follows: During the past ten years I have collected over twenty different recipes from various

sources, tested all of them, and found that any method
which prevented the evaporation from and the penetration
of air into the egg would keep them "good" from three
to twelve months—provided they were stored in a cool,
dry place—but I have never yet found any way to keep
them "fresh" for any length of time, or any method
whereby they could be kept good enough to be sold as
fresh eggs.   I have eaten at Christmas-time eggs that
were packed the previous July, and although they had no
disagreeable taste or smell, they certainly had not the
taste of new-laid eggs; but still they were better than
none, and I doubled my money on a lot of eggs so packed.   I did not attempt to palm them off as "strictly
fresh" eggs, or anything of the kind.   I sent them as
first-class preserved eggs, and obtained the highest market
price for preserved eggs, but that happened to be twelve
cents a dozen less than the price of new-laid eggs.   At
the same time a neighbor sent to the same commission
house a lot of eggs packed according to a recipe that
he paid a "poultry sharp" $2 for; they were sent as
"strictly fresh new-laid" eggs, and as he had been shipping to the same house for a year, and his goods were
always as represented, his mark was well known and the
eggs were not examined as they would have been had
they arrived from a stranger.   He obtained the price of
new-laid eggs and "crowed" over "yours truly" after
the most approved masculine style of doing such things.
In a few days after he received the money there came
another letter from the firm, and it read about as follows: "On the strength of your mark we sold your con-
signment of eggs to some of our best customers; of

course they soon discovered that the eggs were not as represented, and they were returned to us. We have since sold them for what they are—good preserved eggs —and we pocketed the loss on the lot, but we respectfully decline any further dealings with you." I afterwards found that the eggs were packed exactly as I packed ours—except that he paid $2 for the recipe that I picked up in a newspaper. He did not mean to be dishonest; his fault was in swallowing the story of the "sharp," who assured him that eggs so packed could not be told from new-laid. And right here let me say that nine-tenths of the egg-preserving recipes that different parties offer to send on receipt of $1 or $2, or offer as a premium for something or other, have been published time and again in half the news and poultry papers in the country. Some of the fellows who are anxious to get a living some "easy" way—no matter how dishonest it may be, so that it does not bring them within reach of the law—get hold of these recipes, alter the wording a little, and in some cases add another harmless and useless ingredient to the pickle, and then advertise. There is no need for any one who desires to preserve eggs, either for home use or for market, to buy any recipe.

The following method has been patented in England: "Put into a tub one bushel (Winchester measure) of quick-lime (which is fresh-slaked lime), salt 32 oz., cream of tartar 8 oz. Use as much water as will give that consistency to the composition as will cause an egg to swim with its top just above the liquid. Then put and keep the eggs therein, which will preserve them perfectly sound at least two years."

A Western correspondent writes: When it is desired to keep eggs only two or three months, it may be done by using salt alone, taking the precaution to keep the package in a cool place. This is probably as good a method as any to adopt when only a few hens are kept, and it is desirable to retain the overplus of eggs laid in the summer for family use in winter   Take a keg or small jar and cover the bottom with fine salt about two inches thick ; then pack in fresh eggs with small ends downwards, and far enough apart so as not to come in contact, and to afford room for salt all around them. Next put in salt again, filling about an inch above the layer of eggs ; then another layer of eggs as before, and so on till the receptacle is full.   Then cover tightly.

An article written by Mr. Stephen Beale for *The Country Gentleman* contains much on this subject that is interesting.   Alluding to Mr. W. B. Tegetmeier, who was judge of preserved eggs at the late Dairy Show in England, he writes:

"For the purpose of this examination he had been permitted to take away two eggs out of each lot.   These he tested thoroughly, and I give a summary of his remarks thereon for the benefit of your readers.   I explained last week that the eggs had been kept from the 8th of last July to the 8th of October, and as it was at least three days after the latter date before Mr. Tegetmeier could possibly make the examination, the period during which they had been kept was more than three months.   And it is to be remembered that these were the three worst months of the year, namely, July, August and September, and that this year we have had a season of the most intense heat, such as we have not experienced here for many seasons. Therefore, this experiment was sufficiently trying to satisfy the most exacting, especially as the eggs were kept in the offices of the Dairy Farmers' Association, and under no such favorable conditions as would be, the case in the cellars or store closet of a farm-house.

"The lots of eggs entered for this competition were thirty-one in number, and in each lot there were two dozen eggs. Seven were packed in common salt, which in some cases had previously been thoroughly dried. Respecting these, Mr. Tegetmeier says : 'The eggs when broken were alike in quality ; the salt had absorbed a rather large portion of the waters of the albumen, or white, consequently there was a considerable air cavity at the larger end, the presence of which was evident by the sound produced when the eggs were shaken. The white was thickened by the loss of water, but otherwise very little changed, and the eggs were perfectly good for pastry or cooking purposes, being superior to the common shop eggs obtained in London during the winter season, being free from any objectionable odor or taste.'

"It is evident that these eggs would not be suitable for sale, however good in cooking, for the shaking of the contents would be fatal to them in the former respect. One of the lots of eggs packed in salt had been first wrapped in thin paper, but there was no difference in the result. In addition to the seven packed in salt alone, there were three others with which salt was the actual preservative. One of these was packed in sand and salt, another in a mixture of slaked lime and salt, and a third had been first coated with a solution of **gum arabic**, and then packed in salt. But the result was the same in all these cases, as when the plain salt had been used.

"One lot of eggs was preserved by the u.e of gum alone. The plan followed was described by the exhibitor: 'Eggs dipped into a strong saturated solution of pure gum arabic: operation twice repeated. Eggs thoroughly dried, then wrapped in paper and packed in bran; eggs three days old.' This is a somewhat troublesome system, but the result showed them to be well preserved, and the white was more natural in appearance than the previous lots, consequent upon the gum having prevented any evaporation.

"Three lots of eggs had been coated with melted wax or paraffine, but it is remarkable that these were all decided failures. When the wax was removed, the shells were found to be more or less discolored, and on opening, the insides were mildewed, and the contents spoiled. This is all the more surprising, as the lot which won second prize at Birmingham last December was preserved in the same way, and by the same exhibitor as one of these. The system then answered very well indeed, but this time has been a failure. One other lot of eggs had been wrapped in oiled paper, and then dipped in boiling resin, but they were unfit for use.

"Four more had been coated with fat or oil, and one of these obtained a second prize. This lot had been painted over with melted beef and mutton dripping, and then wiped with a cloth. Another had been rubbed well with butter; yet another 'painted with salad oil and packed in sand,' and a fourth also painted with salad oil, but wrapped in paper and packed in flour. Other three lots had been first buttered or oiled, and then packed in salt. All these seven collections had been preserved satisfactorily for cooking purposes, but as no evaporation had taken place, the white was characterized by more tenuity than in those where the pores had not been actually closed. One of those preserved by oil and 'salt was awarded a second prize.

"Three lots only were preserved in liquids. One was in pure lime-water; another in lime-water, with a very small quantity of salt; and the third in the following: 'Twenty quarts of water, one ounce of saltpetre, one pound of salt, six tablespoonfuls of quicklime; boil the water and saltpetre and salt twenty minutes, and pour that hot upon the quicklime; the next day put in the eggs, and keep the pot covered in a cool place.' These lots were well preserved, and very good indeed for cooking. There had been little or no evaporation, and yet the white was less watery than in those preserved with fat or oil. When wiped dry they had just the appearance of shop eggs. The lime-water process is that used so largely abroad, and it would almost appear as if it was the best system. One lot was kept in an egg cabinet, standing small end downwards on perforated shelves. These were fairly preserved. The other lots do not require any special mention.

"Thus it will be seen, that many of the systems used are good for the preservation of eggs, even through a hot, oppressive summer, but only for cooking purposes.

Of course, there are thousands and millions of persons who would be quite content to eat of these eggs. But, they do not realize what a fresh egg is, and its superiority to one even a week old. I had hoped that this experiment would have indicated some system by which eggs could be preserved so as to be fit for table purposes, but this is not so. It does show, however, that there are three or four ways in which they can be kept, even under the most unfavorable conditions, and be first rate for the kitchen."

A correspondent of the *Farmers' Review* writes:

"I have found little or no trouble in keeping eggs so fresh that when used they are as good as the day they were taken from the nest. The whole secret lies just here, viz.: when they are collected in the evenings, they should be placed in an upright position, the small end downward, on shelves with holes made on purpose to receive them, because in this position (and a very important one to success) the yolk does not come in contact with the shell, the yolk, as it were, being suspended in the center of albumen : if otherwise placed, that is, on their sides, the yolk would then come in contact with the shell, and naturally spoil, every egg being porous. The common mode of keeping eggs amongst farmers is either to pack them in straw, saw-dust, chaff, oats or bran, none of which ways will keep the eggs fresh for any length of time; as they will perspire, you must find some method that will entirely close the pores of the egg and keep them closed. My plan was simple and not at all expensive. I melted together tallow and mutton fat, then took wing feathers of the fowl and greased every egg, being careful to replace them in the same position as at first, and kept them in a dry and dark place. By this method you can at any time sell to the grocer or private family fresh eggs, as they do not lose their flavor or weight."

. The *Farmers' Advocate*, London, Ontario, offered a prize for the best method of keeping eggs over winter. The receipt given below took the prize:

"Whatever excludes the air prevents the decay of the egg. What I have found to be the most successful method of doing so is to place a small quantity of salt butter in the palm of the left hand and turn the egg round in it, so that every pore of the shell is closed; then dry a sufficient quantity of bran in an oven (be sure you have the bran well dried or it will rust). Then pack them with the small ends down, a layer of bran and another of eggs until your box is full; then place in a cool, dry place. If done when new laid they will retain the sweet milk and curd of a new laid egg for at least eight or ten months. Any oil will do, but salt butter never becomes rancid, and a very small quantity of butter will do a very large quantity of eggs. To insure freshness, I rub them when gathered in from the nest; then pack when there is a sufficient quantity."

WAX, TALLOW, OIL, ETC.

Much scientific attention has been devoted in France to the preservation of eggs. The leading principle of all processes is the protection of the interior of the egg from the action of the atmosphere, and, consequently, it has long been settled that only the freshest eggs are

eligible for preservation. To the solution of the prob-
lem (says *The Grocer*) of how to prevent the air from
penetrating the shell of the egg, the experiments of such
eminent *savants* as Musschenbroek, Réaumur, and Nollet
have valuably contributed. They all agree that the most
practicable method is to envelope the new-laid egg in a
light coating of some impermeable substance, such as
wax, tallow, oil, or a mixture of wax and olive oil, or
of olive oil and tallow. Réaumur suggests an alcoholic
solution of resin, or a thick solution of gelatine. Nollet
experimented successfully with india-rubber, collodion, and
various kinds of boot varnish. In practice, the most
successful method has been that of Cornier of Mans.
This consists in covering the egg with a varnish, the
composition of which is kept a secret. Eggs are packed on end in sawdust, and it is said will preserve their
freshness during quite nine months in any climate.
Cadet de Vaux suggested the plunging of eggs for
twenty seconds in boiling water in order to coagulate
that portion of the albumen nearest the shell, and then
to pack them in vessels half filled with sifted cinders.
This process—which, by-the-bye, has been well known in
some parts of Scotland for many years—yields excellent
results, but if neglected for but a second or two, the
eggs are liable to harden. The process known as "lim-
ing" in England, and as the Cadet-Gassicourt process
in France, is very popular; on the other side of the
Channel, however, "limed" eggs are never eaten *a la
coque*, but only in the shape of omelettes, etc. Some
preservers claim to obtain better results, as far as the
taste of the egg is concerned, by substituting ordinary

salt for lime. The solution, it is said, penetrates the shell, and so acts upon the organic matter as to diminish its susceptibility to decomposition. The eggs are immersed during several hours. Appert, the Columbus of food preservers, gave some attention to the subject of egg-preservation. His favorite process was to introduce the eggs into a bottle half-filled with bread crumbs to prevent breakages. After carefully corking the bottle, he placed it for several minutes in a sand bath, the temperature of which he kept at 70 deg. For home consumption the French peasantry have for ages preserved their eggs in a very simple fashion. They take a wooden case, or a large barrel, and pack them in thick layers of saw-dust, fine sand, chalk, bran, cinders, or coal-dust, so that they do not touch each other. In the maritime provinces the peasants use layers of ashes moistened with salt water. Both these processes are successful. Drying eggs and reducing them to powder (an invention patented by Chambard in 1852) is another method of preservation that is profitably pursued in France.

A correspondent of the *Country Gentleman* says: "My plan is to take fresh eggs when they are plenty and cheap, and coat them with lard or any other clean grease. I prefer lard. I put a lump in a saucer or anything convenient to melt (not boil); then with a small rag grease each egg."

The *Farmers' World* gives the following, from a correspondent: "Last summer I was induced to try packing down eggs for winter use. I took some sweet, clean kegs, set them in a cool, dry place, with a barrel of powdered dry earth near at hand. In the kegs I placed a layer of this earth, then a layer of eggs, small end down ; then a layer of earth, and so on until the kegs were filled. These eggs were quite good six months after packing down. By placing the eggs small end down the yolk is prevented from dropping down on the end and settling on the shell, while the dry, fine earth keeps them from the air."

GLYCERINE AND SALICYLIC ACID.

The following method of preserving eggs has been practiced to some extent in England :

"Take 5 pints of water, together with 1¾ pints of pure alcohol, add to it 3½ ozs. of pure glycerine, and stir in with it as much salicylic acid as the mixture will absorb. When it will take no more the salicylic acid will show as a sediment at the bottom. Take your eggs, which must be quite new-laid, put them quite clean into the liquid, leave them in it for an hour, and let them dry in a basket. The liquid must not come into contact with any metal, only china, or glass, or wood. It should not come much into contact with the skin. The first time I tried it I treated it quite as if it were water, and a few days afterwards all the skin peeled off my hands. The quantity given will do for many thousand eggs. The moment the eggs have been taken out pour the liquid into a bottle and stopper up well. The eggs will remain good for a very long time. It is the salicylic acid that serves as a disinfectant. Alcohol is used with it, as it is able to absorb a deal of this acid in a liquid state, whilst water will only absorb very little.

"Supposing the eggs were put into this mixture without the glycerine, when drying the eggs the alcohol would soon evaporate, leaving the acid in crystalized dry form on the surface, which would not be sufficient.

"Glycerine has the power of attracting dampness from the atmosphere; it is used for this reason to keep the acid from crystalizing on the surface, and by keeping it liquid and the pores of the egg filled, the egg does not show any outside sign of the treatment. If well done it will keep eggs for months and months, only care should be taken that none crack.

J. M. REYNUAAN, Manager.

St. Leonard's Poultry and Fruit Farm, Ringwood, Hants.

"P. S.—At this time of the year, a very simple way is to butter the eggs, and put them, thick end down, upright in bran, and they will remain good till Christmas."

PACKING IN BARLEY MEAL AND BRAN.

H. Boothby gives a very simple method of preserving eggs, which may answer the purpose very well, put in practice by those persons who only wish to keep a few to the time of scarcity, for family use. It is as follows:

"First obtain some wooden boxes about eight inches square, with lids, then mix barley meal and bran in equal proportions. Put a layer of this barley meal and bran in the box to the depth of an inch, then place the eggs in, end downwards. Put another layer of barley meal and bran, then more eggs (making about twenty-five), and fill up with barley meal and bran. Place a label with the date on the lid, and put the box thus filled in a dry, cool cupboard or other place. Reverse the eggs about once a week, and they will be found in four or five months' time nearly as fresh as newly-laid.

"The way I manage with my eggs is this: I keep ten Brahmas, and nearly all their eggs laid after July I pack away as described above for winter use. I turn them over once a week, perhaps more if I have time, and the supply of eggs will last me till my birds come on to lay again at Christmas. Thus by this simple process I have a fresh egg for breakfast all the year round."

Another man writes: "I pack in a box or in a keg in wheat bran or chaff, small end down. Anything like chaff or cut straw will answer. I prefer bran. I have kept eggs twelve months as good as when put away, and have no doubt they can be kept any length of time."

And still another writes: "Put the eggs into a large pail and pour boiling hot water over them, then put a cover over them and count sixty very slowly. Take them out, wipe dry with a thin towel, and pack with little end down in buckwheat-hulls, oats, or bran. Put in a place where neither frost nor damp can touch them, and they will keep for months. The boiling water shuts up the pores of the egg-shells, and keeps them fresh, while it does not cook them. Another way is to rub each egg over with linseed oil, put on with a cloth. Lay them on a table to dry and then pack away tightly. Lime-water and salt will also keep eggs, but they are not so well kept as by these other methods, as they absorb the salt, and the white loses its freshness and will not beat to a froth or give lightness to cake."

ASHES.

A "Country Rector" gives his method of keeping eggs successfully for a few months. We find it in *The Live Stock Journal:*

"Some time ago I found in the *Journal* a very simple plan of storing eggs in dry ashes, and ever since I have adopted that system with very satisfactory results. Though rather fastidious about eggs, I have frequently eaten and enjoyed eggs that had been in the ash-box for more than four months. But this week I have tested the system still more severely. A box of ashes, that had been used for storing eggs, was laid aside as empty until two days ago, when a solitary egg was found in it that had been laid on May 5th, 1882. Though more than a year old, the egg was perfectly good, and formed part of an excellent pudding the same evening. The only necessary precautions seem to be these: to see that the ashes are quite dry, and to see that the eggs do not touch one another."

SALICYLIC ACID.

Late German papers contain accounts of an experiment made by Schuster on the preservation of eggs, by a process depending on the well-known antiseptic property of salicylic acid, the growth and multiplication of the living organisms which cause fermentation and decay being prevented by the presence of this acid. Fresh eggs that had been packed in cut straw, after having soaked for an hour in a solution made by dissolving 50 grammes (nearly two ounces) of salicylic acid in a little vinegar, and diluting with a litre (about a quart) of water, were found unchanged, both as to weight and taste, at the end of four months; while similar eggs not soaked in the salicylic acid solution, but otherwise treated precisely like the first lot, were spoiled. The method is both simple and reasonable, and well merits the attention of those interested in preserving eggs.

A writer from *Cassell's Magazine* calls attention to the following process for preserving eggs; it has been proved a perfect success by many and careful experiments. On removing the eggs from the nest, they are coated with butter in which two or three per, cent. of salicylic acid has been dissolved, and then they are placed, individually, in a box filled with fine and absolutely dry saw-dust. Care must be taken that the eggs do not touch each other, and that they are completely enveloped in saw-dust; and should these precautions be strictly observed, they will keep fresh for several months, possibly for more than a year.

A simple method recommended by the *Scientific American* consists in the immersion of the eggs in a solution of salicylic acid, prepared as follows: "Dissolve salicylic acid (which costs about $3 per pound) at the rate of a teaspoonful to a gallon of boiling water. It is not necessary to boil all the water; a larger amount of the acid can be dissolved in a gallon of water, and then added to the cold water, but the whole mixture should be at the rate of a teaspoonful of acid to a gallon. This solution must in no case come in contact with any metal. The eggs are kept immersed in the liquid."

SULPHUR.

The *Farmers' Review* gives directions for what is

known as the sulphur process. "Place the eggs in a tight keg, box or barrel, the size according to the quantity of eggs, which should in no case fill it more than two-thirds. On the top of the eggs lay a board and on this place an iron or earthen vessel, in which to burn sulphur. A pound of sulphur is sufficient for a barrel filled two-thirds with eggs. Set the sulphur on fire and cover tightly to confine the fumes and let it stand for an hour. The sulphur fumes being heavier than the air, will sink to the bottom and envelope every egg in the lot. In another box, keg, or barrel place about an equal quantity of oats, or rather more, and treat in the same way. Then pack the eggs in the oats, fill the receptacle full and head or nail up, and turn upside down every day to prevent the yolks from adhering to the shells, and it is claimed that they will keep perfectly sweet and good for a year."

POSITION FOR PACKING.

There is a diversity of opinion on this subject, as on many others. One person has practiced packing his eggs small ends down, and has been successful; while another has packed the large ends down, and has been equally successful in keeping the eggs for months. All agree that it is better that the eggs should not lie in the natural position—unless they are turned very frequently. We may learn the truth in this matter by careful experiments better than any other way. Mrs. Freeman writes in (*English*) *Live Stock Journal:*

Since I have kept fowls, I have always been most careful to keep my eggs as Mr. Lewis Wright advises, viz., the big end downwards; and I maintain that that position makes a most material difference in the quality of the egg. Last year I wanted to give this method a fair test. I repeatedly set eggs which I had preserved for three weeks in the above mentioned position, and they hatched all right. I have also given three-weeks-old eggs—always kept in the same way—to people most particular about their "fresh-laid eggs," and I must acknowledge the gourmands have been "taken in," and paid me all sorts of compliments about my exquisite eggs.

If Mr. Voitellier had given it a few minutes' reflection, he must have himself come to the conclusion that there is a great difference between keeping eggs standing on the big ends, or left to lie in the natural position. When the egg is put on the big end, the whole weight is on its air-chamber, and that is consequently prevented from expanding too freely, and of course the egg, instead of getting stale, is kept fresher much longer. If the egg is kept laid flat the air-chamber can spread with great facility, having no weight to prevent it from doing so.

However, as facts are generally better proofs than words, I beg to say that yesterday I stored three eggs, which will be kept standing, and three more which will remain in the "natural position" which Mr. Voitellier advocates. After three weeks I shall take the liberty of sending them to your office, trusting somebody will have the kindness to try them, so as to be able to give his opinion as to which method of storing eggs ought to have the preference above the other.

And now the result:

It will be remembered that in our issue of March 9th, Mrs. Freeman, of Farnborough, criticising a letter of M. Voitellier's, respecting the preservation of eggs, stated that she had stored half-a-dozen eggs, three of which were to be kept standing broad end downwards, the plan advocated by Mr. Lewis Wright and others, and which she herself had found the best, and the other three on their sides, as advocated by M. Voitellier. These eggs, together with three new-laid ones, were received by us on Wednesday afternoon, and we gave one of each lot to different members of our staff, to be tested by those who were unacquainted with the meaning of the numbers upon them, and who consequently could not be prejudiced in any way.

Mrs. Freeman sent with them the following particulars, the envelope containing which was not to be opened until after the eggs had been tested.

I. Have been kept standing on big end since February 28th (28 days).

II. Fresh laid yesterday, March 27th.

III. Been kept laid flat since February 28th (28 days).

We may add to this that the three marked I. were yellow in the shell, and appeared to be from Brahmas, and the others were white, apparently Minorca, or from a similar breed.

The reports are as follows:

No. 1.

I. Good average egg, nice in flavor, and fairly fresh, but the white adhered to the side.

II. Similar to I., but not quite so good in flavor.

III. The best of all, milky, good flavor, no smell, and very fresh in appearance.

This bears out the testimony of M. Voitellier, so far as the mere preservation of the egg is concerned, but as it is quite possible that III. was naturally richer in flavor than II., that would be sufficient to account for the quality being better.

No. 2.

I. Deep yellow yolk—white pure, and taste good.

II. Yolk not so deep-colored, very fresh, and best of the lot in taste, flavor, and appearance.

III. Strong in taste and smell.

Here the new-laid egg was picked out, but the one kept standing on the broad end was found to be nearly as good, whilst that lying on its side was strong both in taste and smell. This, of course, supports Mrs. Freeman in her contention that the former is the better method.

No. 3.

I. Very fresh indeed, rich in flavor, and without smell.

II. Equally as fresh, but not so rich in flavor. Between these two there was no difference, except that the former was a little richer in quality.

III. Rather stale, not bad, but like an ordinary box egg.

In this also is Mrs. Freeman's opinion supported, as is the statement made by that lady—namely, that she has "given three-weeks-old eggs to people most particular about their 'fresh-laid eggs,' and I must acknowledge the gourmands have been 'taken in,' and paid me all sorts of compliments about my exquisite eggs." Therefore, as we must be democratic enough to allow the majority to decide, the vote is in favor of keeping eggs with the broad end downwards.

Mr. L. Wright's testimony has weight, and we insert it as follows:

"For storing eggs, a very good plan is to have a large board pierced with holes, in regular rows. Many breeders keep them in bran; and this latter method is perhaps best for those meant only to be eaten; but for setting hens the pierced board has many obvious conviences. They should always be kept with the *large* end downward. This direction being exactly contrary to that usually given, we should state that our attention was first called specially to the subject by a most intelligent lady, who advocated this plan, alleging as the probable reason of its superiority: 'Keeping eggs on the small end appears to me to cause the air-bubble to spread, detaching it from the shell, or, rather, from its membranous lining; and after being so kept for a fortnight the air-bubble will be found to be much spread, and the egg to have lost much vitality, though still very good for eating.' She then described her success the other way, adding: 'Owing to this method of storing, such a thing as a stale egg has never been known in my house, and as regards success in hatching, for several seasons, when I was able to attend to my poultry myself, of many broods set, every egg produced a chick." We were by no means hasty in adopting or recommending this plan; but, after careful observation and comparison for two seasons, have proved indisputably that, both for eating or setting, eggs do keep much better the large end down. There is after a week a marked difference in eggs kept in the two positions as regards the spreading of the air-bubble, which is well known to affect both the freshness for eating and vitality for setting of stored eggs, and after three weeks the difference can be discerned even by the taste alone. It will, of course, matter little which mode is adopted, provided the eggs are used for either purpose within a short time; but the longer kept the more the difference from the two positions increases, and, while eggs stored with the small end down cannot be depended upon after a fortnight to produce more than a proportion of chickens, those kept in the way we now advocate will keep perfectly good for hatching a month or even more."

But here comes a correspondent of the *Lancaster Farmer* with a different story:

"It is sometimes desirable to store away eggs in the summer or fall, when prices are so low that we cannot afford to sell them, and keep them till in the winter, when they are often very scarce, and will be keenly relished, or can be disposed of at a good price. To keep them thus we do not believe there is a more simple and efficient way than the one we have always practiced, and which was successfully practiced by my father for the last thirty or forty years. This is by simply taking none but perfectly fresh and sound eggs and setting them in layers on the tip or small end, in a box or basket or anything that will hold eggs. We do not put anything between them, nor do we put them up 'air-tight,' but we always keep them in the cellar.

Eggs that we have put away in this position last fall, are to-day—after six months—as good and as fresh as the day they were laid, and we have never found one that was spoiled or stale among them, when thus served. We feel confident that they would keep good and fresh for one year. I wish some of your readers would try this method and see how long they can keep them, and then report the results."

A Wisconsin housekeeper has preserved eggs fresh from fall to spring by the following recipe : "Take a piece of tough, pliable paper, five or six inches square. Wrap it cornerwise around the egg, and twist the paper protruding at each end of the egg firmly in place. Let the paper be large enough to cover the egg entirely, pack in tub or box, small end down, and keep in a cool place." This secret of keeping eggs seems to consist in excluding the air from them, and in standing them on the little end down, so that the yolk cannot adhere to the shell. Of course eggs should be packed when perfectly fresh, for a change begun cannot be arrested.

Another method for keeping eggs on a small scale, practiced by some people, seems to be a compromise:

"Wrap each egg carefully in paper and place in a bag. Have the bag of strong muslin, and puckered up at one end and tied tightly, with the string left in a fixed loop, so that it can be hung by it. Tie the other end of the bag up close to the eggs, so that they can not move at all, and leave the end of this string in a loop also. Each day reverse the hanging up of the bag, and at the end of six months the eggs will come out as fresh as can be.   The eggs may be put in a few at a time, as they are gathered fresh."

PACKING FOR TRANSPORTATION.

"The great egg season is from March to July. They come usually packed in straw, a layer of uncut straw at the bottom of the barrel, and then an inch of cut straw, and then layers of eggs and straw alternately to the top, which has, like the bottom, uncut straw.   The whole is pressed down with powerful leverage, and on goes the head.   Barrels of eggs are whirled on the chime, and not rolled like a barrel of flour.   The straw for packing is kiln dried and machine cut.   Eggs at this season are all good; later, when hens go into the out-of-the-way places to lay, the eggs are not found for some time, and they do not keep so well, and for the same cause they are better the earlier layings.   A merchant receiving a shipment of eggs, say fifty barrels, has perhaps ten of them "candled," that is, an expert passes them, three in each hand, before a candle.   This is done with great rapidity.   Reclamation is made for damaged or bad eggs, but generally they pass along from dealer to dealer, the loss of the bad eggs falling on the purchaser.   There are various ways of preserving eggs. The one most in use is storing them in immense vats in a solution of lime and salt."—*Am. Dairyman.*

"It is no uncommon occurrence in cities to see a grocer unpacking eggs, many of which have been broken, thus disfiguring many others.   This is a matter to which those who are about sending eggs long distances to market should give the closest attention.   Never use chaff.

Oats are good, but rather costly. Fine cut hay or
straw are the best and most available materials, and
should always be sweet and dry. Put three inches of
this at the bottom of the package, then a layer of eggs,
with the end toward the side of the package, but not
touching the side by an inch or more; then put on
several inches of packing, pressing down gently with a
follower; remove all but an inch in depth of the packing and put in another layer of eggs in the same way
as the first, taking care that the packing is pressed between the ends of the eggs and the sides of the package, and so continue until the last layer is in, which
should be covered with at least two inches of packing
and an inch of hay, and the cover of the package
pressed down closely. Eggs packed in this way can be
transported long distances without injury."—*N. Y. Herald.*

Poultry and eggs are transported in great quantities,
long distances, every season. New York city receives
thousands of car-loads of live and dressed poultry yearly;
and one writer estimates the number of eggs going to
the same destination at 25,500,000 dozens. These eggs
are in great proportion gathered from the farms not near
large towns, at the West. The methods of gathering,
handling, packing, transporting, etc., are important, and
it is no wonder that so many are inquiring to find out
the best methods. We quote from a published lecture
on this subject, delivered by S. C. Gable, as follows:

"Eggs should be gathered at least once a week, and
during the warmer months as often as facilities will per-
mit, and should never under any circumstances be left
standing around, exposed to the heat or flies. All egg

shippers, whether large or small, should carefully candle their eggs, especially during the warm weather, and if any seconds, such as dirty or stained eggs, they should be left out and packed separately from those which are to comprise extras or first quality. When eggs are carefully candled, and all fresh eggs packed and shipped at once, the loss is comparatively light. But it is not profitable to ship stale eggs, as they will be rotton before reaching their destination; neither is there any benefit in paying freight on rotten eggs, and such are the ones that cause losses, and sometimes make a great deal of ill-feeling between the shipper and receiver. From my own experience, when a shipper in former years, I always found it the most profitable to ship eggs as long as they could be marketed to good advantage, and during the warm months I could not ship too often. My advice is to ship eggs when fresh, and as often as possible. As there are a great many shippers who hold the eggs, which are gathered during the latter part of September and the month of October, I would advise them to use only the best and cleanest oats, which should at least be a year old. Rye is the most cooling, but not being raised on a large scale, and more expensive, I find old oats the next best thing. Before packing up the eggs the oats should be run through a fan, so as to be entirely free from dust or any such dirt usually found in them. These eggs, after being held in oats, before they are put on the market in the late fall, should be again candled and repacked in prime cut straw or wheat chaff, for then they will present a better appearance, and are more salable. While the eggs are held in the oats there are always some that will get rotten, and if shipped to market in the oats there is generally suspicion, and the cry of 'ice house stock' is raised, even if they are not such.

"Guinea eggs, or keats, as they are termed in the Western States, should especially be packed in separate packages, for if packed in with hen eggs the buyer will insist on having them at the same proportion as cracked eggs, or half of the price of sound hen eggs. When we receive guinea eggs that are separately packed, we have always a trade to take them at about two-thirds of the price of fresh hen eggs. Guinea eggs, when mixed with the hen eggs, are very often the cause of a great deal of trouble between the buyer and the seller, and I think if the egg-shippers of the West would combine themselves, and make up a 'shooting match,' and use nothing but guinea hens for the occasion, and destroy them all, it would eventually make the egg business a little more profitable to themselves.

"In regard to packages for shipping eggs, we, in Philadelphia, like New York, prefer barrels, but from what I can learn Boston, Chicago, and other markets prefer cases. We prefer the barrels for various good reasons, but principally because they are more adapted for sending eggs to out-of-town trade, such as watering places, and our coal and iron-mining districts, where we could not possibly send cases, unless we were to keep several thousand on hand just for that purpose; and to empty and re-case the shippers' eggs would be an enormous amount of labor and valuable time lost, especially in the spring of the year. For packing, we prefer clean, fine-cut rye straw, although wheat straw will also answer. Barrels should be uniform in size and style, and new barrels always add to the appearance of a shipment, even if it is only a small lot. The eggs should be packed uniform, the same number of dozens in each barrel. A great many Ohio shippers use a 30-inch barrel for packing eighty dozen, and when properly packed these carry very well, but far Western shippers should not pack over seventy-five dozen to the same size barrel, or, better still, use a 28-inch barrel, and only pack seventy dozen. In regard to packing the eggs, we can hardly say much, for we find the prominent Western shippers have very good experience in packing. I must say that some have one great fault; that is, in heading up their barrels they are pressed too hard, and invariably there are a few mashed eggs in the first and second layers; this presents a very bad appearance to the buyer, and very often some good sales are missed, and even the reputation of the brand is hurt to a certain extent.

"I have found the pickling vat and the ice-house the only successful means of preserving eggs, but I must give the latter mode the preference. The ice-house steady temperature of 36 deg. to 40 deg., although eggs will keep in a temperature of 40 deg. to 44 deg. All eggs for cold storage should be perfectly fresh and thoroughly culled."

EGGS COMPARED WITH MEAT.

The food value of eggs and the cost of egg food has not been properly considered. In fact, the public in general put a low estimate on the nutritive value of eggs, and have a mistaken view of their cost. The *Scientific Farmer* meets these mistaken views when it says: A dozen of average sized eggs may be assumed to weigh a pound and a half. If we calculate the food value of meat and eggs, as force producers—that is, the amount of work they oxidized in the body are theoretically capable of producing—we have 990 foot tons for the pound of lean meat; and 1284 foot tons for the pound of eggs. As flesh producers a pound of eggs is about equal to a pound of meat, as the following analyses show:

ONE POUND OF EGGS.

	Ounces.	Grains.
Water	12	36
Albumen	2	..
Extractive	..	130
Oil or fat	1	214
Ash	..	28

will produce, in the maximum, two ounces of muscle or flesh.

ONE POUND OF MEAT.

	Ounces.	Grains.
Water	8	...
Fibrine and albumen	1	221
Gelatine	1	62
Fat	4	340
Mineral	..	350

AGE AND QUALITY.

Do not accept any unnecessary risk. Simple means are at hand in every household to distinguish bad eggs. There may be good eggs, doubtful eggs, and bad eggs, all in the same basket. Place those that are at all doubt-ful in a vessel of water, deep enough to allow the eggs to float—if they will. Those foul and musty with age will stand on end, the small end, too, as persistently as if held there by a magnet; but good ones lie quietly at the bottom of the dish, and thus the good and bad can be more readily separated than in most circumstances in life. Of course no really honest person will sell eggs, the freshness of which is in the least doubtful, when he can so easily practice this simple method of assuring himself of their integrity.

It is very annoying to the good housewife to break an egg of bad odor into her cake or custard; and when hurried, one is apt to forget the usual rule, which is, always to break each egg into a cup by itself, so that the good ones may not suffer, like Dog Tray, by being found in bad company. Still worse is it when bad boiled eggs, supposed to be fresh, find their way to the breakfast table, and to the egg-cup of the fastidious visitor.

Under this head we add a few sayings from the *Rural Gentleman:*

A good egg will sink in water.

A boiled egg which is done will dry quickly on the shell when taken from the kettle.

The boiled eggs which adhere to the shell are fresh-laid.

After an egg has laid a day or more the shell comes off easily when boiled.

A fresh egg has a lime-like surface to its shell.

Stale eggs are glassy and smooth of shell.

Eggs which have been packed in lime look stained, and show the action of the lime on the surface.

Eggs packed in bran for a long time smell and taste musty.

With the aid of the hands, a piece of paper rolled in funnel shape and held toward the light, the human eye can look through an egg, shell and all.

If the egg is clear and golden in appearance when held to the light, it is good; if dark or spotted, it is bad.

The badness of an egg can sometimes be told by shaking near the holder's ear, but the test is a dangerous one.

Many devices have been tested to keep eggs fresh, but the less time an egg is kept, the better for the egg and the one that eats it.

PICKLES AND PRESERVES.

Wisdom is found in proverbs. They resemble sharp-shooters, who are apt to hit the mark. There is something more to be said about "egg pickles" and those "valuable recipes" which are advertised all over the country. The man who buys a recipe for preserving eggs, merely on the recommendation of the vender, without proving its efficacy, would be classed by the leading author of proverbs a fool. There is no *secret* pertaining to the preservation of eggs, that is worth buying. The best methods have been published in the agricultural papers and the poultry publications so that they are the property of every man who desires to use them. Yet there are always some new fish that never felt a hook, and they bite when a bait is presented. We just found in *editorial advertisement* in this line which we insert in part, as it is a specimen brick. In this case the inventor sells a "pickle" instead of a recipe for making a pickle, and in this he is cunning. Names are omitted:

"We have heard of a great many ways to preserve eggs for future use, but have never come across anything equal to the process used by Mr. P. He sent me in October, some eggs preserved by his process in April last, and we have examined them carefully, and must confess they were the best preserved eggs we ever saw. They looked as well as new-laid eggs, and we defy any one to detect that they had ever been in pickle. On breaking them into a saucer they kept their shape, were perfectly sweet and not the least smell of age about them. They cooked like fresh eggs, and in taste and looks we could not discover but what they had just been laid. Mr. P. is very enthusiastic over his new process for preserving eggs, and well he may be, for it is something that has long been sought for, and now, it being a settled fact that eggs can be preserved for an indefinite period, it will add hundreds of thousands of dollars to the wealth of the nation. But farmers are the ones who are going to reap the greatest benefit from it. Instead of selling their eggs at from six to fifteen cents a dozen they can pack them and hold until a favorable market calls for them.

"Mr. P. is considered a straight and square man among his neighbors, and they are willing to endorse him. He does not sell this receipt, but does sell this pickle in a concentrated form so that in ordering it from him it requires only a small quantity to produce a barrel of the pickle in which you can preserve some seventy or eighty dozen of eggs. This process has been in use by Mr. P. for several years until he has brought it to that state of perfection that it seems impossible to improve upon it."

That may be a very good pickle: it may be as good as any other. It may be sold from house to house like yeast; and if the seller should own some good layers of fair eggs and should take some, fresh from the nest, as samples, would not the article sell among honest farmers like "hot cakes"? It would be wrong to decry a valuable invention, but there has been much false pretense in this matter of preserving eggs. Let no man pay for the privilege of making his own lightning-rod; for we read that Franklin made the invention long ago, and it is free.

A FRENCH METHOD.

During the seige of Paris, when that city was so hemmed in by the German army that the country poulterers could not get their eggs to market, neither could the Parisian go out except by the agency of a balloon; it became a matter of great importance to preserve the fresh eggs that were already in the city, especially those necessary for hospital use. Of course this was done with the best art and science that was available in the French capital.

The method, as described by a French newspaper, was as follows: Pack the eggs in carbonized bran. First put in a layer of this material one inch thick, then place the eggs, ends down, with space between them sufficient to prevent coming in contact with one another, then another layer of bran one inch in thickness, then eggs again in the same manner.

Eggs preserved in this way were kept fresh, and used in the hospital for the sick and wounded; and, though several other methods of keeping eggs were used, none were as satisfactory as this. We can perceive no reason why bran prepared in this way would be at all superior in preserving effects to powdered charcoal. Carbon has a quality that preserves meats, and we read that poultry was preserved in the same manner as eggs in the French hospitals. Ordinarily it would be easier to obtain ground charcoal than carbonized bran, but the latter would not blacken the materials packed in it as much as the fine dust of charcoal.

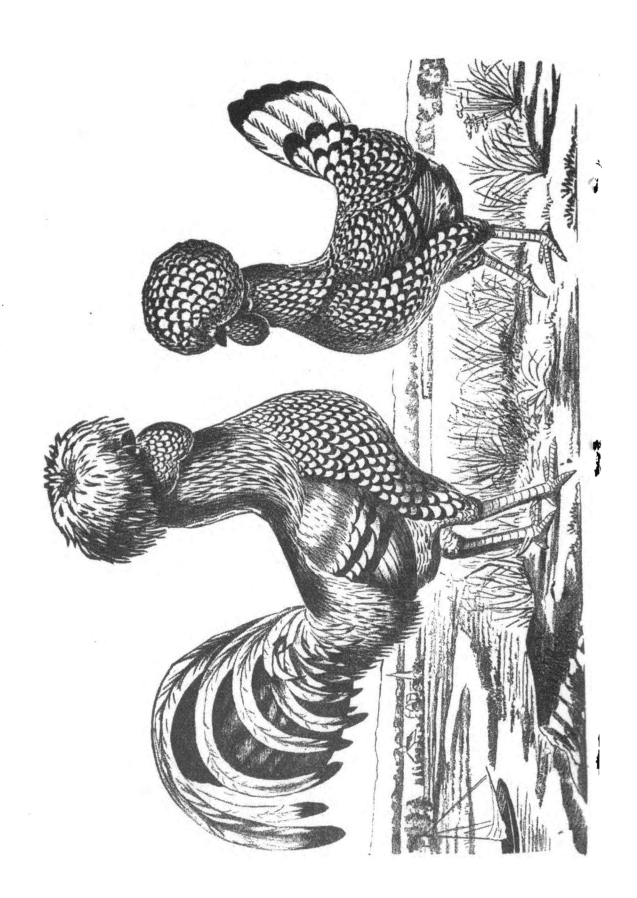

Made in the USA
Las Vegas, NV
24 October 2024

10433249R00033